Necessary
Schizophrenia

Necessary Schizophrenia

A Caregiver's Memoir

Calondra Stickley

MℲM
Mirembe Hollow Media

This book is lovingly dedicated to

Kelley Lyle Rubio

Melanie Welivar

and Robert Stickley

who also lost their mothers to cancer

Introduction

C.S. Lewis said, "We read to know we are not alone." This is the story of the time in my life when I felt most alone. It is the story of my life, intertwined with my mother's life, as she battled cancer. My hope is that you will be able to relate to some of my feelings and experiences, so that you will not feel alone in your journey.

This story is comprised of two parts—the journal I kept during my mother's illness and my thoughts now, as I've gone back, remembered, and filled in some details.

There were a lot of hard days. There were a lot of mundane tasks related to caring for mom and I wrote about my frustrations with those kinds of days. But mostly, I wrote about the "other" things I did during this time, because I needed to remind myself that *my* life was still going on.

Fall, 2000

Saturday, September 23, 2000
Fairfax, VA

"Aunt Cali, what do you want to be when you grow up?" asked Anna.
"Um, I don't know yet," I replied.
Anna was seven when this conversation took place. I was thirty-three. What's wrong with this conversation? Isn't it supposed to be the other way around . . . the adult asking the child what she wants to be when she's grown up? I guess it's a compliment, since Anna didn't see me as being a grown-up and all.

I'm having a bit of an identity crisis lately. About the whole grown-up thing and what I want to be. It's been over a year since that conversation with Anna, and I still don't have a clue. I've thought about several things. Tried several things. Decided which things I don't like being. I'm struggling with who I am more than anything. My friend John described me as a necessary schizophrenic. How is that possible? Let me explain . . .

My mother is dying of cancer. She's been sick for quite a while, but in September the doctors finally found the tumors that were making her so sick. My family is very close. We got even closer. We came together as a family to beat this thing. This disease. This enigma, which seems to strike randomly and go into remission randomly. The doctors could not remove any of the tumors, and mom chose to treat the disease holistically. She chose alternative medicine. We stood by mom, and her decisions. We prayed a lot. We fought hard. We were going to win this battle.

Wednesday, October 25, 2000
Barnes & Noble – Reston, VA

I am full of emotion today. I feel as though I could sit with a pen and a notebook and start writing and never stop. I haven't eaten today. It hasn't seemed particularly important. I'm starting to get hungry. I don't want to waste my time with food. I haven't written much in the last several months. My words got stuck. Or my pen fell asleep. It didn't have the energy. I didn't have the energy. I still don't, but now it's become necessity. I am a writer. I am many things. But today I am a writer. Today, I bought a new journal to write in.

Looking back, who could have known the words that would eventually fill these pages? If only I had known then, what I know now . . .

Six weeks ago, I moved from Virginia to California. I've wanted to move there for several years. I packed my stuff and put it in a U-Haul and moved. We drove for eight days, then I was in California for eight days. I spent two of those days on the beach, walking in the ocean.

The day after I arrived, as we were unpacking the truck and moving all of my possessions into my friend's garage, I got a call from my mom. She told me that she had been admitted to the hospital the night before for emergency surgery on her colon. They put in a colostomy, and that process had gone well. And then she told me that they found cancer. A lot of cancer. Too much to take out. And they stitched her back up again.

Of course, I was shocked. I felt like I should go back to take care of her. She assured me that she was going to be fine, and that she would let me know when there were any changes, or when they received more information.

A week later, I was in Old Navy buying a black shoulder bag, on clearance for $3.99. My phone rang. Dad said mom wanted to talk with me. Mom was crying. "Please come home," she said. So I did. Caught a red-eye flight home that night.

I'm back in Virginia now. It's fall. The leaves are all changing colors. Last October mom and I went to Maine to see my friend Kari. Rhonda, Kari's sister, has cancer too. Rhonda is having chemo. My mom is not. That's okay though, because mom is still going to get better.

I'm tired of telling people why I'm back here and that my mom has cancer. Today I've had my first day of solitude since I came home six weeks ago and that's been good. Necessary.

Mom seemed to be getting better. She was going to be okay. She was going to be a cancer survivor. This disease was not going to beat her; she was going to beat it.

I was in Virginia for four months during the fall and winter of 2000-2001. My mom was a fighter and she really focused all of her time and energy into getting better. I returned to California in January 2001, confident that she was going to be well again.

California, 2001

So I picked up my life where I had left off, which happened to be right smack dab between two chapters, so the break was almost unnoticeable. I started the new chapter of my life in a new house in a new state with a new career and a few old friends, but mostly new ones. Things were going well until mom called from the hospital . . . the cancer had spread.

It was mid-June, and my first feeling was anger. I was scared. I needed to see her. I got on a plane and flew back to Virginia. She had been having trouble with her chest cavity filling with fluid. This was compressing her lung capacity, making it difficult for her to breathe. The doctors were able to drain out most of the fluid, but it began building up more frequently, and we couldn't figure out why it was happening or how to make it stop. It was really scary, because the doctors were saying that she may only be with us for a few weeks or a few months. I didn't know what to do ... whether to stay (until when) or whether to go back to my new home. After talking with mom, we agreed that I should go back to California. I would come home for a visit at least once a month. I needed to continue moving forward . . .

Saturday, July 7, 2001
Encinitas, CA

This is the story of my life.
I've learned that it is constantly changing
And that can be scary sometimes.
The events of my life change me
And influence the me I am;
          The me I thought I knew;
          The me I'm becoming.
I'm not the same person today
That I was yesterday.

These are the things I know
FOR SURE:
1. Jesus loves ME
2. Love is the most wonderful thing
3. Love is the most painful thing

4. Family is important
5. My mother has cancer
    and I love her . . .
6. The ocean is good for the soul

I walked and walked and walked in the ocean
today. This is my time to get in as much ocean as
possible. Before I go back, whenever that is. I know
I have to go . . . I know it's not now, but soon . . . I
just don't know when. And what am I supposed to
be doing in the meantime?

Waiting is difficult . . .

Here I wait
And be.

I spent hours and days by the ocean, often alone and occasionally with a friend. Walking. Sitting. Just taking in the sound and the smell. I sincerely believe that the ocean is necessary. It is healing. It is, truly, good for the soul.

Wednesday, July 11, 2001
Encinitas, CA

The sky has no clouds today

Just miles and miles of
 . . . blue . . .
Like the ocean.
The saltwater ocean.
Like saltwater tears.

There have been many today.
Mama's in the hospital having her lungs drained
again. Nobody seems to know how to make the
fluid stop coming. This is not good, and I don't
know how to make it better.

I just don't understand.

Saturday, July 14, 2001
Encinitas, CA

Today was a p.j. Saturday . . .

        Tea on the front porch
        Talking to my friend on the phone
        Trying not to think about a boy I like . . .
                . . . unsuccessful
            (but a nice diversion)

Last night was overalls and flip-flops
And dinner at Filibertos with my friend Kevin . . .
A long walk on the beach with fireworks,

glowing waves,
twirling,
arm in arm
A long talk in the hammock,
6 things I know to be true
my mama
me
A fun movie at home,
And a bear-hug goodnight.

I laughed much last night. That was very good.
Kevin is comfortable.

Today was slow. Good slow.
And peaceful.

Jesus, I will rest in you.

Summer, 2001

Tuesday, July 24, 2001
Walter Reed Army Hospital

It's Tuesday and I am back home again. I flew in
yesterday and came straight to the hospital to be
here with mom. I'm glad I'm here. She's being
discharged today. This is good.

Undated
Fairfax, VA

I put my life on hold again. Not because she asked
me to, because she didn't. Not because I thought
she wanted me to, because I didn't. I did it for
selfish reasons. I did it for me. Because it was
necessary. Because I couldn't be all the way out
there, in California going on with my life when she
was in Virginia and hers wasn't going on so well.

15

I came home. We talked. We cried. We prayed a lot. We continued to fight hard. And here is where I am. Being a necessary schizophrenic because on one hand I am here with her helping her fight the hardest battle she's ever fought. Encouraging her. Telling her that it's going to be okay. And on the other hand, I am watching her die. I am mentally trying to prepare for my biggest fear to come true. I keep telling myself that if God chooses to take her home, it's going to be okay. Even when it doesn't feel okay.

And as I sit and wait for her life to play out however it will in the days ahead I have become very introspective. And insecure. And uncertain of most things that I once believed to be true. I've lost myself along the way, and these are my thoughts. My questions. My wonderings and wanderings. My search not for who I want to be when I grow up, but for who I am now. Because that person will be enough.

"People travel to wonder at the height of mountains, at the huge waves of the sea, at the long course of the rivers, and they pass by themselves—without wondering."
– St. Augustine

Monday, July 30, 2001
Fairfax, VA

I've been home for a week. There have been good days and not-so-good days. Today is right in the middle.

Saturday was a good day. We went on a family picnic to the Kenilworth Aquatic Gardens. It was beautiful! Then we came home and sat out on the back porch all evening and ate and talked and laughed. Mom felt good.

And the day's big announcement was that the new baby's name (my niece who is due in December) is going to be Sara Lynn.

Kenilworth Aquatic Gardens is tucked into a back corner of Washington D.C., and most people aren't aware that it's even there. This was one of mom's favorite places. It's a "magical" place, with water lilies, Lotus flowers with their huge bowl-shaped leaves, frogs and lizards, butterflies and bumblebees. And if you have an ounce of imagination, you can see fairies sliding down the Lotus leaves, into the clear pools that collect in the middle.

What was memorable about this day was that, apart from us pushing mom in a wheelchair, it was a "normal" day. Most of our time was spent fighting cancer, going to various therapies and doctor's appointments, but on this day, she embraced the day, and just lived!

Thursday, August 16, 2001
Fairfax, VA

Today was conflicting.
> It was difficult.
> It was frustrating.
> It was relaxing.
> It was renewing.
> It was wearying.

Yesterday . . . mom started chemo.
> She did great.
> Today, she's not so sure.

Her body is fighting against her spirit.
She feels sick and she's very depressed.
I try hard not to take what she says personally.
This is not so easy.
I don't know how to help her.
Taking care of her is wearisome, but *she* is not.
She is the reason I am here.

The decision to start chemo was a very difficult one for mom. She continued seeing her homeopathic doctors and therapists, integrating what they were doing with the allopathic doctors and the chemo. Her hope—our hope—was that the combination of the treatments would be strong enough to make a visible difference in her health.

I had lunch today with a friend from my old job. Then I went to Barnes & Noble and found Sabrina Ward Harrison's new book, *Brave on the Rocks*. I read it, from start to finish. This was a very good, and inspiring thing for me to do. It cost $23 that I didn't have so I didn't buy it. She listens to my favorite band, Over the Rhine, who was in concert last Tuesday night in Arlington. My brother, Keith, and I went. The music was, as always, captivating.

During my time home last fall we all realized how important it was for me to make sure I had some time to myself. It's a really tough thing to make happen. Almost impossible. It feels selfish. But it too, is necessary. I found that if I didn't get time away, I was much less effective in my ability to care for mom. Not so much on a physical level, but on an emotional level. And cancer is an emotional disease. Yes, the physical aspect is difficult, but I believe the emotional aspect is the most critical. Tuesday was my "day off." I usually ran personal errands and then went to Barnes & Noble to read, write, and drink coffee. I felt comfort in being surrounded by books. I also participated in a Bible study on Tuesday evenings. After Bible study, I usually went over to my brother's and just watched TV. It was good to just do nothing for a while.

Sunday, August 19, 2001
Barnes & Noble – Fairfax, VA

There is rain outside today. It didn't start out rainy but now there is a drizzle. I feel like a drizzle. So the rain suits my mood.

Keith said, "Just pick something and do it Cali. You can always change your mind later." I know he is right but it is still hard. There are always excuses to not try, but . . .

This comment from my brother came because of my unending analysis of trying to figure out what my purpose in life is. What I am going to be (when I grow up). In my life it is still constantly changing . . .

What I do know is that this is my story, and it is important to write it down now, because somewhere along the way I started getting lost. I keep finding my way again. So I know I'll always figure it out eventually, but during the lost, it's a little bit scary. Right now it's a little bit scary.

Do people want to know my story? What will my story add to the world? How will it touch them?

For two days I have not been able to deal effectively with frustrating situations. I get upset. I try to reason with her. I try to explain. I say, "It's not my fault." I get tired of trying to predict, or figure out, what mom will want and/or how she will want it done. I feel like she is too hard on Papa. Too nit-picky. He's doing the very best he can and she won't let that be good enough. She makes me feel like I'm the only one who can do it *her* way. That is a LOT of pressure. Especially when it's not true. I can't be everyone . . . I can only be me, and I don't even have a good handle on who I am right now. I am defined by my mother and her disease. I don't like that, but somehow I chose it. I know this doesn't make sense.

I keep telling people I'm sorry. I feel like I'm letting them down. Or that I'm not "super-human" enough. I shouldn't have to apologize for being human. For having feelings. For not being enough. I don't like myself when I feel this way.

There is so much irrationality with cancer. I'm not sure what causes this. When you're in the midst of the situation, it is very difficult to realize that it's not the person you love that is attacking you, and the way you do things. It's the disease, causing the irrationality.

At least the drizzle outside seems to have ended. Temporarily . . . Life is temporary. The sun is trying to come out.

For a change, I want someone to tell *me* that it's going to be okay.

"She had hoping eyes
that looked further than she knew."
– Sabrina Ward Harrison

Was my hope visible in my eyes? I hoped so.

Wednesday, August 22, 2001
Barnes & Noble – Fairfax, VA

Decaf, grande, two-pump, soy mocha. Starbucks. And Barnes & Noble. This is good.

Yesterday mom saw the Chinese herbalist from Chicago. He told her to quit everything else . . . all other treatments . . . (just like all the other doctors always say) . . . and just do his treatment. No more chemo. It makes her too weak. Just his treatment, and don't expect fast results. Be patient . . . it may take several months. I'm afraid she doesn't have several months. Does anyone realize how critical this is?

I cried again yesterday. I feel like I'm watching her die. She doesn't know this is how I feel. She keeps saying, "When I get better . . . ." I'm afraid to hope for when . . . because I think I'll be devastated if that doesn't happen.

> *I was afraid to share my feelings with my mom. I felt like she had so much on her plate already, that she didn't need to be listening to my fears and worries. I always tried to stay positive around her. Always tried to encourage her. Did I do this because I was trying to help mom feel better, or did I do it to protect myself from my worst fear coming true?*

I called Kari one night last week. Her sister had breast cancer, and surgery, and a year of chemo—all last year. She is in remission. But Kari knows. She understands how it changes a family. How difficult it can be. How scary. How tiring. How confusing. She just knows. She said she would come help if we needed her. I love her.

Mom was extremely protective of the people that she allowed to be around her. She usually felt that when someone new came into her home that they were looking at the things she had and making judgments about her based on her things. It was almost like she thought they came, not to see her, but to see what she had. This is an example of one of her irrationalities. After I talked with Kari, mom told me that Kari was welcome in her home any time, because the first time Kari came to visit, Kari focused on her, and didn't make any comments about her house or her things. She was wary of other people and while she was reluctant to let anyone new into her home, she seemed to let almost any homeopathic professional in, without question.

Monday, August 27, 2001
Fairfax, VA

On Friday, Keith brought over Anne Lamott's book *Traveling Mercies.* I've been reading it and it touches me, in my soul, and makes me want to write. Inspires me to share my story. I think this is a good thing.

I woke up on Friday with a pain in my right side. A familiar pain. Ovarian cyst pain. This was not fun. It hurt much more than the previous one. I took Percocet to dull the pain and it dulled me. I was feeling a little better yesterday evening, so of course I overdid it today. But the house is very clean and looks good.

When someone in your house has cancer, it is the only illness. No matter what the pain or sickness, it's never as bad. So you take medicine and you keep going. You do whatever you have to do to push through. I'm not saying this is the best way or the only way; it's just the way it was in our lives. A caregiver's job is never-ending . . . and who takes care of the caregiver? You are the only one who can take care of yourself. It is no one else's responsibility. Maybe that is why it is such a difficult thing to do . . .

Mom is having more and more difficult days. She is carrying approximately 50 lbs. of fluid and it is affecting her energy, her ability to walk, her ability to get in and out of the car, her ability to do just about everything. She's much worse than she was when I came home five weeks ago. It doesn't seem like five weeks already. It's getting harder and harder for her to keep fighting. Harder to do most everything.

Sunday, September 9, 2001
Fairfax, VA

Ah . . . the frenzy. The hectic pace. The tiredness.
This life. My life. So closely interconnected right
now with my mom's life. And her life is waning.
This is life. And the sheer exhaustion of it all. There
is necessity in writing. And it's been difficult here
again these past couple of weeks. Some really hard
days—emotionally and mentally. Coming to grips
again with what is happening. Even though my
head is constantly aware, my heart lives mostly in
denial in an effort to protect me, I think. Usually it
works.

I went to Lynchburg last weekend. Stayed with
dear friends. I had coffee with Mrs. Delong, one of
my former professors whom I adore. I saw so many
friends, and shared meals with them. It was my
weekend away. A time for solace. I'm so glad I
went.

I stopped and saw aunt Ruth on my way home.

*Aunt Ruth was my 99-year-old great aunt. She
was living with my parents until they had to move her
into a home, as mom was no longer able to take care of
her. Aunt Ruth also had dementia. She had always
been so sweet, and truly a lady in every sense of the*

word. I loved her stories. She became a Christian at the age of 98. My mom led her to the Lord. Ruth Doolittle Ackland passed away just 6 days shy of her 101st birthday, on September 7, 2002.

When I got home from my weekend trip, I walked in the front door and nothing was right. Everything was wrong. This was extremely difficult. I was up till 3:30 am trying to help make it better. Her anger is so irrational.

Coming home from that weekend away was one of the most difficult times my mother and I experienced. Maybe one of the most difficult times for my Papa and Keith as well, since they had been taking care of her while I was gone. In a sense I felt like we were all punished for my going away. Like we had done something wrong. But that was not truth. One of the things that we talked about and cried about (after we finally stopped yelling) was her need to see us express emotion. Mom felt like we were just going through the days doing our new "job" of taking care of her and treating it just like a job. We were working hard trying to make sure she was all right and had everything she needed, physically. What we didn't give her was the emotional connection of expressing our feelings to each other, visibly. She didn't see us sad or crying. She

27

said it was necessary for her to see that this affected us emotionally. To know that we were sad or tired or scared. We talked for a long time that night. I cried and cried. Her hair was falling out in clumps. And instead of me telling her it was going to be okay, like I'd done for months, she held me while I cried and told me it was going to be okay. Even now I can't write about it without tears coming to my eyes. I miss her so much.

Mom's red blood count was too low, so there was no chemo on Wednesday. This would have been her second chemo treatment. The chemo nurse recommended that mom have a blood transfusion, so the day was spent having lab work done in preparation. Thursday, mom had muscle testing by the homeopathic doctor all day. Friday morning, she went in for her blood transfusion at Walter Reed Hospital. I went to the hospital after lunch and stayed overnight. We were able to arrange for mom to have a CT scan on Saturday before coming home.

Being able to arrange for mom to get the CT scan was really an answer to prayer. Because her primary medical focus was on homeopathy, she was not having traditional diagnostics done, so there was really very little factual information available to allow us to monitor her progress. Really, mom's health was based only on how she was feeling. The lack of testing allowed us all to stay in denial about whether her condition was getting worse.

Mom is very possessive of me. She's afraid that no one else can (or will) take good enough care of her and that they won't treat her gently enough. THIS IS VERY HARD! It wears me out. I can't be everything she needs . . . even though she thinks I can.

It's so difficult for me to get time away on my "day off" and still get enough sleep. Often, by the time I am actually able to leave, it is around 5 pm. The day is mostly done by then. So I drag it late into the night. This is not good for me, but it's the only way I know how to do it.

Hospice is coming on Tuesday. Hopefully this will make it easier for all of us. Hopefully, she will let them do their job instead of asking me to learn it and be them, too (like her massage therapist, her acupuncturist, her homeopathic doctor, etc.). I hope my expectations are not too high.

The talk that mom and I had when I came home from my weekend away bonded us more closely than before. I don't regret that for a minute. But I still felt pressure to be the one who did everything for her. The decision to allow Hospice to become part of her care was significant, given her distrust of people. I really don't know who convinced her that it would be good to add them as part of her care. I just knew that my hopes were very high regarding the relief that I would feel as a result of having their help. Honestly, they were involved for such a short time before she dismissed them from her care routine, that I barely have any memory of them at all.

Please let this week be less emotionally difficult. Please.

Sunday, September 9, 2001 (later in the day)
Fairfax, VA

And so I decided that I am going to be . . . a writer.

I told this to two people this week who don't even know each other. They both said, "Do you want to write essays or novels?"

It doesn't really matter . . .
I just need to write.

Tuesday, September 11, 2001
Fairfax, VA

Today, America changed forever. The twin towers of the World Trade Center are no longer standing. Each had a hijacked, commercial plane fly into it. The Pentagon was also hit by a passenger plane. And another one crashed in Pennsylvania believed to be headed for The White House. It's hard to believe.

This was a catastrophic day in America's history. Of course we were all affected by it. My mom worked for Continental Airlines, at Washington Reagan National Airport. This had been her career, and her friends who worked at the airport were directly affected, as the airport is very near the Pentagon. When the airport closed for a month, these were her friends that were out of a job, not knowing if they would ever work in that building again. These terrorists had been planning their strategy for several years and my mom told us that she had actually boarded some of them onto planes in the past. She said that you never forget a face when it just stares right through you. She recognized their faces. And those faces haunted her, more than we realized, I think.

Another aspect of that day, for me, was that yes, it was a very tragic event, and many lives were lost, but what about all of those people, like my mom, who were also fighting for their lives? What about all of the people who die from cancer every year? The numbers are higher, but few people talk about the tragedies that are going on, on a daily basis, in individual lives all around the world. Life is hard, but not just for the families who lost loved ones on 9-11-2001.

Autumn, 2001

Wednesday, September 20, 2001
Fairfax, VA

Guess what? I figured out today that I *do* have an occupation right now . . . I'm a caregiver. That's what they call it, and that's exactly what I am. And you know what else? I'm good at it! But that doesn't mean I have to do it forever. And it doesn't mean I can't be something else at the same time, like a writer. Why is it that we crave titles for definition in our lives? I'm not sure, but for some reason, it gives recognition to what we do. What I do.

Mom had her second round of chemo on Monday. It went well, all things considered. It's the days that follow that are most difficult. This is day three and her spirits are good and that, it seems, makes all the difference. Hospice started last week, and that looks as though it's going to be a really good thing—very helpful and informative. Somehow it takes a level of pressure off of me to know all the doctory-nursey answers. There's someone to call when we need help!

Kevin, my friend from California, called me on Sunday because we hadn't talked in a while. Mom said it was good to hear me laughing. He's good at that—making me laugh!

Aunt Ruth turned 100 on the 13th. We had a birthday party for her last Saturday at the Olive Garden. It was very nice. She seems very happy!

I rented *One True Thing* on Tuesday night. It's a story about a single girl who moves home to take care of her mom who is recently diagnosed with cancer. Yeah, there were many similarities, but enough differences. Still, it made me cry, but I'm glad that I watched it. It helped in some weird way.

I think this helped me, because I knew that somewhere, someone was able to relate to how I was feeling. I know it was "just" a movie, but someone wrote that movie, and that person understood.

Mom's hair loss isn't bothering me as much as it did when it first started to fall out, but she's still got a lot left. We haven't had to shave it off yet. I don't know how that will affect me. But it will be okay, right?

So I don't feel as aaaaaggghhh this week as I have lately, and I'm glad. It comes in spurts, like everything I suppose. But I feel like I can "handle" it right now and I'm glad. We're learning balance. That's a good thing!

God is taking care of us all!

Tuesday, September 25, 2001
Fairfax, VA

Last week was good for me. I feel like I figured out a bunch of things in my head.

This morning Erin, my sister-in-law, and I drove out route seven, up to the shop at Hill High Orchard for coffee and lunch. We enjoyed the drive and seeing the colors of the changing leaves. We both bought these cute little Gnomy faeries!

The Gnomy faeries are small figurines, made in Holland, which we discovered in the shop there. Our purchases that day became the start of a special collection in our family.

It was my day off, and I actually got out of the house early. Hill High is an orchard with a unique little shop and eatery. Mom and dad had discovered it several years ago on a fall day when they were on a drive, enjoying the colors of Autumn. Mom had been reminiscing, and sharing that story with us earlier in the week, so Erin and I wanted to experience Hill High Orchard first hand.

I crocheted two hats this past week for mom. She looks so cute in them and she loves them. All of her hair hasn't fallen out yet, but it's so thin and coming out so fast. One hat is burgundy and the other one is white. My niece, Amanda, wanted to learn to crochet, so I'm teaching her, and she loves it! The next thing I'll make is a black chenille scarf for myself.

I started knitting and crocheting again while mom was sick. I found it was something that I could do while we were together, or even when she was sleeping and just didn't want to be left alone. It was something that, most importantly, I could put down quickly when she needed me.

Mom has lost 10 lbs. of water weight this week. That's a really positive thing and I think that's helped her to have a much better, more positive attitude this week. She feels like the chemo is working.

I am lonely. I wish there was someone who would be with me through this, even though that is difficult. I want mom to know him before she is gone. And then I want to marry him.

Mom shared with me, one afternoon while we put together a puzzle, that she always had a sense that she would never know the man I married. I realized that, as difficult as it was going through the experience alone, it would have been almost impossible for me to come home to do what I did with the responsibilities of a husband or a family. In hindsight, I realized that this fact alone might have been the reason why God had allowed me to remain single. I know God always has a plan and a reason, but that still didn't take away the loneliness.

Tuesday, October 2, 2001
Fairfax, VA

This past week has been amazing in many ways, but mostly with mom. She actually seems to be getting better. I'm glad. Relieved. But scared to believe. Scared to be hopeful. Scared that it's not really coming true. Cautiously optimistic, I suppose.

On Thursday, after mom's appointment with her homeopathic doctor, she didn't want to go straight home. So we drove out to Hill High, where Erin and I went last Tuesday. She walked in all by herself and she didn't have to use oxygen, so that was something to celebrate. We ate egg salad sandwiches and cheesecake, which were not part of her normal diet! And to continue the new tradition, we each bought a new Gnomy faerie.

On Friday, she said she felt so much better. Last week was full of "mostly better" days. Good days. Amy Maudlin's wedding reception was on Saturday afternoon in North Carolina. We asked mom if she wanted to go? I told her I'd drive her—she did great going all the way out to Hill High Orchard.
"Really?"
"Sure!"
"You think I could?"
"Absolutely!"
Keith rented a big car. We packed lots of pillows. We drove mom to North Carolina! Amy was so surprised and Linda cried. It was a good trip all around. No negatives to it at all. We did it! Mom did it!

We knew, Keith, Papa and I, that this was one of the best things that we had done. Keith and I had spent lots of time talking and were concerned that all of mom's life was caught up in doctor's visits and remedies and routines designed to help her get well, and that she wasn't experiencing moments any more. She was working so hard to get well that she'd stopped experiencing joy in the now. Taking this trip was something that was completely focused on her giving joy to someone else. Amy is the daughter of one of mom's best friends, and this trip meant getting to see Linda, and congratulate Amy. I still am amazed, looking back, at how well she did on that trip. She was so happy!

Thursday, October 4, 2001
Fairfax, VA

On Tuesday mom and dad celebrated their 40th anniversary (which was actually on Sunday). They went out for Chinese food and then drove to Harper's Ferry, WV. Of course they stopped at Hill High Orchard on the way back home. They bought a special Gnomy for their anniversary.

Wednesday morning mom still felt so good. But by Wednesday afternoon she felt so bad. Wednesday evening mom said, "Call 911," and on Wednesday night mom was admitted to the hospital. Her bowels have stopped working. She's having severe spasms in her stomach and she's been throwing up a lot. Yesterday it was all bloody and that scared me. Today she has a tube through her nose draining her stomach. It's not bloody anymore. They're not sure what happened or what's wrong. They want to do a CT scan tomorrow. Obviously, her intestines are blocked. She's really praying that the blockage will open up and start moving so they don't have to do surgery. That's her biggest fear. I understand. It's scary. She's on Dilaudid for pain and that scares her because constipation is a side effect. So she's hesitant to use it, even though she really needs it.

At this point, mom had been a hospice patient for three weeks. It was definitely helpful having them involved in her care. However, because of her admission to the hospital, she had to sign out of hospice. She was eligible to re-enroll, however, because of the "insurance red tape" she decided that it just wasn't worth it. It was very important for her to be involved in the decision-making process regarding her health and her care. She felt that hospice did not

allow her to make these decisions for herself any more.
She continued to be very untrusting of most people.

I was hoping to go camping with my friend Saturday night, but I think the doctor is planning on keeping mom through the weekend.

I just don't know what's going to happen . . .

Tuesday, October 8, 2011
Fairfax, VA

So mom got to come home on Friday night. The blockage opened up at about 3:00 am on Friday, which was a huge answer to prayer. She felt so much better on Friday.

Sunday, October 21, 2001
Fairfax, VA

I'm very tired tonight. There are many elements of today that have made it very tiring. But there was so much good in today too.

Tuesday, October 23, 2001
Fairfax, VA

Last Tuesday I drove to Richmond. It was sunny
and warm and autumn. I drove with the windows
down and the radio loud. That's why I didn't hear
the pager going off until I got to the top of the exit.
It said 2727, which was our emergency code for
ASAP. Call home ASAP.

I had driven down to meet Patrick, face to face, for
the first time. His mom was diagnosed with cancer,
stage four, thirteen days ago. She'd been in the
hospital ever since. Patrick ordered "the machine."
The normalizer. An alternative treatment for curing
cancer. I was going to go with him to take it to the
hospital when it arrived.

> Patrick and I had a dear, mutual friend, and he and
> I been phone friends for a couple of years, but we'd
> never actually met, face-to-face. He had been praying
> for my mom's healing. This was an opportunity for me
> to do something to help him.

I arrived at his mom's house, where we planned to
meet, and he was just like I imagined him. Of
course, I'd seen pictures, but I *knew* Patrick. And
he looked plumb adorable. Just like the Patrick I
know. We hugged. And then he told me his mama

had died just after noon, while I had been driving down. That was what the 2727 was all about. His mama. Not mine.

Sadness.

I'm so sorry . . .

Of course it's not fair. Life isn't. But God works it out. His way. And His ways are higher than our ways. "The machine," said Patrick, "I want you to take the machine." Shock. Surprise. Overwhelmed. "Take it home to your mom. I want her to be able to use it. I'll get it back later." "Are you sure? I don't know what to say." and I said that because I didn't know what to say. I was overwhelmed. Patrick . . . giving to me—not just a machine, but more importantly, giving me back my hope . . . that is a priceless gift. I came to encourage, to support, to give . . . and I walked away with hope. A gift of friendship . . . an offering of love closer to my heart than any gift I've received. This is God's love, manifest.

The normalizer . . . "the machine" . . . was an electronic device that had been found, in some studies, to be an effective alternative treatment for cancer. It was extremely expensive. Mom used the machine almost every day from that point on.

So Friday was the U2 concert in Baltimore. I went with my brothers. It was my early Christmas present from them. It was great. And very different from the San Diego show, which I also loved. This show had a different energy. A passion. A purpose. A message to communicate. A feeling to share. It was part of our mutual need to process what had happened on September 11. A time to celebrate our unity, our fears, our hopes. The band played *Kite*. Bono said he wrote it for his kids, but that since his dad had died 2 months ago, he thinks maybe his dad wrote it for him. The night that mom told us how sick she was, last June, Keith and I played *All That You Can't Leave Behind* in the car as we drove all around DC. I cried the whole time they were playing *Kite*. The song about goodbye. The concert as a whole touched many places in my heart, and it was full of energy, and full of purpose, and full of God.

Tuesday, November 6, 2001
Fairfax, VA

I am compelled to write if for no other reason than to feel the smooth paper underneath the skin of my warm hand and sense the monotony—the wonderful rhythm—of forming letters and words and sentences.

I am fascinated constantly at the immense power of language—the ability of letters to form words, words to form sentences, and sentences to express the inner depths of the soul—the essence of a person's being—for another to share.

I am amazed at the inadequacy of letters, words, sentences to fully express the depths of the soul— and therefore thankful for music to complete the process. Music—it's own language.

There is, truly, passion in living life.

Thursday, November 8, 2001
Fairfax, VA

I'm not sure why I'm having a difficult time with myself here lately.

I'm restless again.
Fidgety.
Tired and bored.
I hate this feeling.

On Monday I cleaned the house and then I went to see *Serendipity* with my friend while dad took mom to get her lab work done. My brother, Norman, and his girls came over and I cooked dinner. After dinner I helped mom get set up for a tea party with the girls. Then I cleaned my room.

The tea party. Mom had been talking about it for weeks . . . wanting to have a tea party with her granddaughters. They had done it once before. They dressed up and put on jewelry. And hats. Of course, you can't go to high tea without a hat! I just didn't quite get it. I had missed the first tea party. I tried to discourage mom. "You're tired. You've had a long day. It can wait till next week when the girls are over. We'll plan for it," I said. But she wanted to do it then. I was the one who was tired. I had had a long day. I wanted to plan for it. I didn't want to be making little sandwiches and cheese crackers and slicing apples after I'd cleaned house and cooked dinner. But she was determined. So I helped her get everything ready. I got dress-up clothes for the girls. And jewelry. And hats. We set up a small table in the living room, got out a fancy tablecloth, and set up the tea party. I served the ladies while they talked about the weather, and books, and told stories. They stepped into the world of make-believe and magic happened in those moments. The one thing my nieces all talk about when they are remembering their maw maw is her tea parties. I didn't understand then. I do now.

Tuesday I spent here, at Barnes & Noble like I usually do on my day off. I prepared for Bible study and then read a very fun book: *Ella Minnow Pea*. It's a funny, fictional story about letters and words and language.

Yesterday I made a spreadsheet with all of mom's lab work results since July. Then I called Kevin and he helped me write the proper formulas to chart each blood count so we could have a visual image of where the levels are now compared to the past few months. I was pleased with how it turned out.

When I say I was pleased with how it turned out, I mean that I was proud of the job I had done constructing the charts to represent the data. I was discouraged though, by the results. I didn't like the results, and what they represented. I tried to approach the whole thing non-emotionally, but that is difficult when there are visual results telling you that the condition is declining.

And Ed came on yesterday.
My favorite TV show . . .

This show was one of my escapes. It allowed me to be somewhere else, in an imaginary world, where cancer wasn't killing my mom.

I haven't felt so well lately. Mom's doctors all tell me that I should use "the machine," or I should get on their program, take some supplements—and I'll be fine. Okay, whatever.

Sure—I'm always fine. It's in my nature, I guess. No matter what, I'll always be okay.

Thursday, November 15, 2001
Fairfax, VA

Mom, dad and I went to Williamsburg on Tuesday and got back today. It was a pretty good trip, overall. Mom was sick Tuesday night but had a great day on Wednesday. She felt really strong and walked a lot. And not slowly either. The drive back today seemed short. I got to see my dearest friend, Karen and her daughter Lauren. They met us at the hotel yesterday and we got to visit and catch up.

Mom did so well on her trip to North Carolina that she wanted to try a short trip to Williamsburg. Her great day on that particular Wednesday was the last, best day she had. Somewhere after this trip, she started going downhill. We all believed that she would bounce back to what had become her "normal" like she always had before. It didn't happen.

Tuesday, November 19, 2001
Fairfax, VA

I've been having a bit of a difficult time these past few days, but today I feel somewhat better, so that's good. I've been having severe cramps in my stomach that wake me up, they hurt so badly. I had four "episodes" in eight days and that was a bit scary, because I feel like there is sickness in my body, but I don't know what it is. I hope to be getting insurance next week and then can go to the doctor to get some tests done. I'll be glad when that happens, because then I'll know what I'm fighting. It's always easier to fight when you know what you're battling.

It turned out to be my gallbladder. It was 2 ½ years before I was able to have surgery to have it removed. I haven't missed it for a second!

I've dreamt of my home in California two times in the past week. I miss it. I feel a bit homeless at the moment. I also dreamt that my hair was brown again. So since I can't go home yet, I dyed my hair brown. I like it.

Keith and I watched the meteor shower on Sunday morning. We saw about 80 shooting stars . . . it was gorgeous!

Holidays were always a big deal for our family. Mom loved a celebration! A few days before Thanksgiving, she decided that she wanted to do shopping for the big meal. I think it had probably been about 6 months since she had been in a grocery store. We went to Whole Foods for the turkey and all the fixings. I remember helping mom get out of the car, and into the wheelchair, and then heading for the store. There was one sidewalk ramp nearby, and a local radio station had parked their van directly in front of the ramp. The only way to get onto the sidewalk was to go up, over the curb. I was furious, internally, at their lack of thought and subsequent insensitivity. It was not a good start to what turned out to be an extremely long, tiring day. The store was packed, the lines were long, the wheelchair was bulky, and mom seemed to second-guess every decision she tried to make. I wanted to just skip Thanksgiving that year, because it was so much work on top of everything else. But Mom needed Thanksgiving to be a "normal" holiday, and she wanted to celebrate it as we always had. So that is exactly what we did.

Friday, November 23, 2001
Fairfax, VA

Hello.
Alone.
I crawl into bed with crisp, cool, cotton sheets.
They don't stay cool too long.
But I do wish I had someone
To crawl in next to.
Not just someone.
There are lots of those.
I want my own husband
To snuggle next to.
This teddy bear just doesn't quite do.
Hello.
Alone.
Hellone . . . ly.

Thursday, November 29, 2001
Fairfax, VA

Christmas music. Christmas lights. Christmas
smells. Some years the season seems so much
more pungent than others. I'm soaking up the
season with unseasonable temperatures this year
and loving it!

Last night I talked to dad for a short bit. It made me sad because he doesn't feel that mom is really getting better. Maybe he's right. It's confusing when you just don't know who to believe, what tests to believe, etc., especially with no "true" confirmation of progress like CT scans or such. I don't want to believe that all of the "mass" in her abdomen is tumor and not fluid, but it does make sense, and is she stronger now because she stopped chemo, or because the normalizer is working? It could be either. I don't know . . . she wants to go to Mississippi for Christmas, so she can see her mama and her siblings. I hope she can.

I love coffee and books and stars.

Saturday, December 8, 2001
Fairfax, VA

Saturday in December. Crazy. Cloudy. Raining. Grey.

Mom and I didn't have a good week. We fought a little bit every single day I was home. We're both tired and worn out and weary and that's just not a good combination. I hate it.

I cried on Tuesday. And Wednesday. I talked to Kevin Wednesday night after I was done crying. He's a good listener. I seem to have been blessed with many friends who are good listeners.

Thursday I told Lisa that I'm coming home in January . . . to pack my stuff and put it in storage.

Lisa is my friend and former college roommate. We moved to California at the same time, and were roommates again there.

Last night we rearranged the living room to make room for the huge poinsettia that mom's friend brought over. I quite like it, and it will be our Christmas "tree" this year.

Sunday, December 16, 2001
Fairfax, VA

I realized today that tomorrow is exactly three months (!?!?) since mom's last chemo. I remember someone (mom?) asking the doctor, "If I don't do chemo, how long?" and his replying, "About two months."

53

When mom started using the normalizer, she really started feeling better. Because her original decision was to treat this disease holistically, she wanted to give the normalizer a chance to work, and not combine it with chemo. She had a total of two chemo treatments before she decided not to have any more.

Does this mean that all the bad she's feeling is because she is dying? All the books, all the doctors say do this, do that, but what do you do when you've been doing this and that and she is still getting sicker and sicker—each day, sicker?

This was a really disturbing realization for me.

Tuesday, December 18, 2002
Fairfax, VA

Tonight was the last night of bible study for the year. We finished our book. The last chapter was about "How big is God in your life?"

One day in mid-December mom and I went Christmas shopping. She was going out less and less. But on this particular day, even though she didn't feel particularly well, she decided she wanted to go

Christmas shopping. We bundled her up, helped her into the car, and put the wheelchair in the trunk. She and I went to the mall. She had asked me for a little help doing some shopping online, but today she was shopping for the girls. She picked out clothes and gifts. The mall was crowded. Christmas music was playing. We stopped at Starbucks and had special holiday-blended coffee. Coffee was on her list of "not alloweds," but this was Christmas, so she enjoyed every drop! We shopped until the mall closed, and then went home tired, but satisfied with a job well done. She told me she knew this might be her last Christmas.

Thursday, December 27, 2001
Fairfax, VA

We made it through another holiday.
That is an accomplishment.

It's particularly noisy in here tonight, in Barnes & Noble on the Thursday night after Christmas. There are lots of college students and it is distracting instead of relaxing.

The days have become more difficult. Mom is
having more "discomfort" which is her word for
pain.

Mostly bad days.
Lots of tears.
Much frustration.
Very, very tired.

Winter, 2002

Thursday, January 3, 2002
Orange County, CA

I'm at El Torito Restaurant on MacArthur Blvd.,
right across from John Wayne Airport. I'm meeting
my friend for dinner.

I flew into San Diego yesterday. I walked down to
Moonlight Beach and sat in the sand for a while. I
called mom. She's just so sick.

I've missed California. I'll be packing all of my
things in a crate, which will be delivered on
Saturday and picked back up on Monday. I'll feel
good when I know everything is packed up.

*Mom and I sat out on the front porch with a blanket
one morning in December. I told her that I
thought I should go to California and pack up my*

stuff and drive my car home. She didn't want that. She said that I had waited so long to move to California, and she didn't want me to move back because of her. We did agree that it would be best for me to go back, pack up my things, and put everything in storage. I really didn't know when I would be moving back.

Friday, January 4, 2002
Encinitas, CA

As sure as the ocean.

Something in life must be as sure as the ocean.

God, maybe.

The waves are big today . . .
Crashing
Crashing
Sea spray
In seafoam green.

It changes color, the ocean.
And today, it's seafoam green.
And you can see the spray as the waves begin to break.

Waves, the most beautiful brokenness on this planet.

Wednesday, January 9, 2002
Cleveland, OH

Very early in the morning in the airport in Cleveland . . .

I'm on my way home.

It doesn't look like she'll make it much longer.

***

Friday was packing day and basically uneventful.

And Saturday the crate arrived. And Seth, Lisa's brother, arrived. And Kevin came over. I packed in the morning. And after the crate was delivered, Kevin and I walked down to the beach. We sat on the top of the piled sand, and we talked some. And listened to the ocean some. And sat . . . content to be, for the moment.

I had to put my toes in, and it was Pacific Ocean cold, in January. But you know how it is. Just stay in long enough and you'll adjust. We walked in the ocean. Oh, how I missed the ocean. I needed this more than I realized.

Seth helped me pack the crate on Saturday night and I packed the kitchen before I ran out of energy and went to bed on east-coast time.

Sunday I was up early and packing more and then went to Coastline Community Church with Seth. We talked about God in the process of our lives and how we could never make it without Him. At church again that night we sang and worshiped and I cried and cried and cried and God said, "I love you so much and it really is going to be okay."

Sunday night mom called me and said she didn't think she was going to make it until I came home and I told her that was okay. Because that was the right thing to say. And it would have been okay. She's so tired and she's in so much pain. I asked if I should come back home right now and she said not yet. I cried some more.

On Tuesday Keith called because dad said, "Come home." So here I am in Cleveland, almost home— for whatever happens next.

And I'm scared, but I know God loves us all and it really is going to be okay.

Peace . . .

Wednesday, January 16, 2002
Fairfax, VA

My mom went to heaven on Monday.

Sara Holland Ludlow
February 12, 1946 – January 14, 2002

It was her smile.
The way her face lit up and her eyes sparkled.
It's the one thing she had on right until the very
end.
Her smile.

It was her spirit.
The tenacity with which she lived life.
The way she expressed her feelings to her very
core.
Her spirit.

It was her sense of adventure.
Her delight in anticipating the unknown.
Her ability to delve into a new situation with such
excitement.
Her adventures.

It was her family.
Husband, daughter, sons, granddaughters, sisters and brothers.
Just one group of people who love her with all our hearts.
Her family.

It was her friends.
So many of you who honor her today.
Those kindred spirits with whom she shared her heart.
Her friends.

It was her outreach.
The way she was "mom" to so many of our friends.
Her genuine desire to share the gospel of Jesus with those she met.
Her outreach.

It was her love.
Love that she gave with all of her being.
The thing that makes our memories of her so sweet.
Her love.

I didn't write much about mom's last weekend. I have only spoken of it a handful of times over the years. I was with her, right until the very end. And even though she was sedated, she knew I was with her. My friend *Danelis* came to visit, and to help out that last weekend. She pitched right in, helping however she could. She cleaned the house while we were at the hospital. She took care of me. She gave so unselfishly.

Monday, January 28, 2002
Fairfax, VA

It's been two weeks.
Doesn't seem like it.
I've managed to keep my days busy. Filled with people. Which seems to be what I need right now.

Tuesday, January 29, 2002
Fairfax, VA – 6:00 am

I turned out the light at 1:10 am. Woke up at 2:38 with that same old pain in my stomach and got up. Dad was up . . . couldn't sleep . . . anxious . . . fluttering inside. Grief manifest in physical feelings.

We talked about a lot of things. Fears. Uncertainties. "Am I going crazy?" Keith came over. Because we're doing this together. Individually, but together. Each in our own way, but supporting each other all along the way. All the way through the process.

This is something that we actually talked about immediately after mom died. We knew enough to know that grief affects each person differently and that there isn't a right or wrong way to grieve. We agreed that we wouldn't judge each other, but that we would be there for each other, no matter what, all the way through. We're still committed to that. Losing someone you love isn't something you ever "get over." You just keep re-adjusting. I think it is a continual process. One of the best things I learned is that feelings are never right or wrong. They are just feelings. Feel what you have to. Then, act responsibly.

Sleep is induced by medicine tonight and even then it does not come easily. But my body is no longer in pain and I feel a sense of calm relaxation. Restful, even in the absence of sleep.

There is much to say. Even the simple recording of daily events passed over these recent days and weeks . . .

But as sleep lumbers in, I will submit to it. As the full moon sets, and the sun begins to rise.

Wednesday, January 30, 2002
Fairfax, VA

Today dad and I went for a walk . . . over the fence
. . . through the neighborhood woods . . . and back
up our neighborhood street. Then we set out on
some errands. And we went to Arlington National
Cemetery to visit mom's grave. We brought
flowers. A Continental airplane flew overhead.

*Because my papa retired from the Air Force, both he
and mom were able to be buried at Arlington
National Cemetery. It is close to the airport where
mom worked. And from their gravesite, you can see the
Air Force Memorial rising high into the air. How
appropriate . . .*

Tomorrow morning Erin is coming over so we can
start going through mom's clothes. This will be the
first of the "going through . . . "

*This wasn't as difficult as I imagined it would be.
We tackled it like any of the difficult jobs that needed
to be done. Of course, years later, I find myself re-
sorting things that I kept. Each time I do it, I
am able to let go of more and more. It is an emotional
process, but a healing process as well.*

Sunday, February 17, 2002
Agricola, MS

I am in Mississippi at Grandma's house. I arrived on Friday, about lunchtime.

But first, a bit of catching up . . .

We sorted thru the clothes, then we sorted the kitchen. Finally, we sorted most of the big room upstairs. We felt like we got a lot accomplished.

After the sorting, two Fridays ago, I went shopping and bought myself a tanzanite ring . . . from my mother. It's beautiful!

Dad gave us each some money that was left in mom's personal checking account. I wanted to spend mine on something "from my mother" that I would have forever, as a visual, daily reminder of her and her love for me. I still wear it every day.

Saturday, the 9th we had a family celebration to remember what would have been mom's 60th birthday. We had pancakes, with pancake mix that mom had bought on her anniversary trip to Hill High Orchard. We started working a puzzle (something she loved to do), and looked at pictures and reminisced. And of course, we had cake and ice cream!

Then on Sunday morning, a week ago, I started my trip south.

Lynchburg was my first stop. I stayed with Danelis. We went to a Truth concert on Sunday night. They sang *If You Could See Me Now*, which has become a very special song since mom died. It was very touching.

I visited my friend Reva on Monday and on Tuesday I headed south down Route 29. I stopped in Lexington, NC for some really good barbecue with Ralph and Margaret Walker, who were friends of mom and dad when they lived Marquette, MI and then again in California. They knew mom and dad just after they were married and knew me when I was just a little girl. We had a great visit!

Charlotte was my next stop . . . to see Linda and Duke. It was so relaxing to be there. We talked and laughed and cried. We told stories. We remembered. We ate at Cracker Barrel—the same one we ate at in September with mom when we went down for Amy's reception. Tuesday was mom's birthday . . .

Linda sang at mom's memorial service. She and mom became friends back in Tucson, AZ, when they were both pregnant. When I was in high school, I knew if I ever needed to run away, that I would go to Linda's. Over the years, she has become like a mother to me. Her home is always a place of solace when I need mothering!

I left there on Thursday morning for my longest driving day. I listened to the Mitford books on tape—we had started reading them to mom last fall—and they made the miles pass so quickly!

I arrived at Grandma's on Friday around lunchtime and I'm having a wonderful visit!

I was at Grandma's in Mississippi for a week. It was the farthest road trip I'd taken by myself. I thoroughly enjoyed it. On my way back home, I stopped in Lynchburg and stayed with Danelis for about a week. Her mother died unexpectedly about three years before mine, and since she was with me during my mother's last days, I knew she really understood how I felt. This was a very integral part of my healing. Just talking, crying, and laughing openly with someone who really understood. I remember spending an entire day sitting on the floor, putting a puzzle together, on a low table. This gave my mind something to do besides think about how much I missed mom.

Thursday, March 14, 2002
Fairfax, VA

Ah . . . there is much to say. And it seems, little energy with which to do so. Much to catch up on. But it seems that will have to wait.

I sprained my ankle again. The last time it happened was in December, and I learned that acupuncture is *the* answer for sprained ankles.

When I sprained my ankle in December, I was unable to put any weight on it at all. I've had many sprains throughout my life, and it has usually taken about a week, with lots of rest and ice and elevation, to heal to the point of bearing any weight. I was very concerned about how I would be able to continue taking care of mom, and still take care of myself. Before my mother got sick this would not have been a concern, but the irrationality of the cancer didn't allow for anyone else to be sick.

Thankfully, we had an acupuncturist who came to the house once a week to give mom treatments. When she arrived, she told me that she could have me walking without crutches in an hour. I've had enough experience with sprains that I had absolutely no faith in this treatment. However, I let her put two needles in, and an hour later, I was walking. By the next day, I had no swelling and was walking with absolutely no pain at all. Really, this was a blessing from God, to allow me to be able to continue taking care of mom.

The days pass quickly.
Soon, I will be leaving to go back to California.
It seems it is coming a bit too soon.
But it is necessary, I think . . .
So is sleep . . . for now . . .

Tuesday, March 19, 2002
Fairfax, VA

This has been difficult. It's raining outside. I'm at Barnes & Noble. My place. I think it is supposed to rain when I come here to write. It wasn't raining when I left home.

It's foggy in my life these days. And it's hard to focus when it's foggy on the inside. On Sunday, I cried. I hadn't really been able to do that. Not really. Oh, there were little bits here and there. But not really. No, not really. It's part of the process of course. Healthy. Even good for me. Necessary for healing. Rain for the soul, I guess.

Up until this point I had been able to keep myself busy, and surrounded by other people and other things. Once I started crying, I thought the tears would never end. From this point on, tears flowed freely, and it was impossible to predict what would cause them to start again.

If you want to be a writer, first, be a reader. I keep trying to do both, but I can't quite focus. The fog is too thick.

Sunday, April 7, 2002
Fairfax, VA

Sleep eludes me tonight.

With wind outside, blowing the trees,
        Rattling the windows,
        Then silence.

Tick-tock-tick-tock-tic-toc-tic-toc . . .
Racing thoughts
               Empty head
Full head (head cold, ears won't *POP*)
Then nothing.

Tic-toc-tic-toc-tic-toc-tic-toc

12:13 am
I want to sleep
I am overwhelmed

Back and forth
               Alternately
hot – cold
               full – empty
       calm – overwhelmed
racing – silent
               whoosh . . .

Wednesday, April 10, 2002
Fairfax, VA

Counting down the days
And things to be done
Before I leave for California.
Yesterday I printed out old pictures

That I brought back from Grandma's
And had scanned into the computer.

And I had dinner
With my brothers
At On The Border.

Papa and I went to Hill High
And ate blueberry pie
And bought Gnomys.

I was invited by my friend Becky to come stay with
her in central California for a few months. I decided
that this would be a good plan for returning to the west
coast. My plan was to rest and to work on this book.
Then, I would go back down to southern California
and re-establish myself down there. Get on with my
life. Move forward again.

Spring, 2002

Wednesday, April 24, 2002
Manteca, CA

I arrived at Becky's a week ago yesterday.
I finally did it. It was difficult. But I'm glad I'm here.
I'm all settled in. I feel like I belong. Her family has
made me feel very welcome.

I haven't really done any writing, though that was
my intent upon coming here.

But that's okay. It's just not ready to come out yet.
It will when it's time—I'm certain.

I talked to papa today. I miss him a lot. I knew I
would.

I bought a blanket at a craft fair on Sunday, with
some of my "special" money from mom. It's white

and it's the softest blanket I've ever touched. It's very special. Like my ring.

Thursday, April 25, 2002
Manteca, CA

Last night I slept so well. I didn't realize how poorly I'd been sleeping until I woke up from such a good night.

Today I've been on the verge of tears most of the day. That's okay though. Necessary.

Saturday, April 27, 2002
Manteca, CA

Yesterday I cried. Tears . . . a necessary part of the healing process.

Wednesday, May 2, 2002
Manteca, CA

Barnes & Noble. Stockton, CA. Sporadic tears today. And the fog . . . these hours of inability to focus. This feeling in my body that I'm not really . . . what . . . I don't know. This process of grieving hurts in ways that nothing can ease the pain, and intended comforts essentially intensify it. My heart aches. I'm in a daze. Living, but not really. Just moving through this time doing whatever. The tears are comforting and disturbing simultaneously. I know they are necessary. They are like poison burning my skin as they leave my body, and I know that they must leave for healing to occur. But it takes so much energy to cry and today I have so little. I don't want to be alone, but I don't want to be with anyone either. I am a paradox. An oxymoron.

Mother's day is coming and in every store there are reminders and I hate seeing them and yet I'm unexplainably drawn to them. To remembering. My eyes fill with tears again and my heart is torn.

I never anticipated how difficult mother's day would be for me. All of the store displays were reminders that my mother was not alive any longer.

It feels like fear. Yes. C. S. Lewis noted that in *A Grief Observed*. It doesn't make sense, but it is true. I have become overwhelmed by uncertainty. I feel so out of my element, but I don't know what my element is or where to find it or how. My life can presently be summarized by the phrase, or response, "I don't know."

Friday, May 3, 2002
Manteca, CA

This was the first time I was able to look back and write part of my story. Chronologically it goes back to January 14. It just took a while to get it out.

I had to go to the store . . . several stores that day, actually. There were so many little things that had to be done . . . had to be purchased . . . had to be arranged. It was a blessing really. Duties to be done, to occupy my time. But they didn't really occupy my mind. In every store I was surrounded by other people. People living "normal" days. Shopping for things they needed. Even the same things I was shopping for, but for different reasons. I noticed other people more during those first days and weeks. Maybe because I wanted them to notice me. To see me. To know my life had just experienced a terrible, permanent tragedy and I was now a completely different person. Looking back now I couldn't tell you anything about any one person that I took notice of during those days. And if they had taken notice of me, they would have thought the same things of me that I thought of them. I wanted to stop each person and tell him or her. I wanted a t-shirt they could read, and see, and know. I wanted to scream. I wanted the whole world to just stop, because mine just had, but I couldn't stop. I couldn't yell. I couldn't tell them, each one, that my mother had just died.

Tuesday, May 14, 2002
Manteca, CA

Sunday was mother's day. It was my first mother's day without my mother. On Saturday morning Becky and I drove down to Los Angeles. We got an excellent on-line rate for a room at the LAX Crown Plaza hotel. We checked in, made pb&j's and packed the picnic basket. We drove to Santa Monica Beach and ate lunch. We played in the sand. We searched for periwinkle shells. We laughed. Hard. We rested. We listened to the ocean. We breathed in the salty air. We basked in the peaceful calm of a sunny day at the ocean. It was wonderful.

Back at the hotel we got ready to go see Over the Rhine in concert at the Knitting Factory on Hollywood Blvd. We walked through the new Kodak theatre and around Hollywood. We sat at

Starbucks and talked. Then we went to the show. It was captivating. It touched my senses. The sound of the familiar music shared with people I love. It was a wonderful evening.

I planned on skipping church but felt compelled to go. A friend invited me to go to church with him. God met me there. He spoke to my heart. He used the pastor's message to confirm what He's been telling me—to run to Him—to rest in Him. To be, just be, with Him. He's healing me. Moving me through this process and using my loss to bring me into closer fellowship with him. I asked Bill to pray for me. And I cried—healing, necessary tears.

Becky and I spent Sunday at the ocean too. It was more crowded. We saw a seal. We didn't stay long. We took the Pacific Coast Highway north, through Malibu, up to Ventura. Somewhere along the way, at a remote spot of coast and rocky beach, we stopped. I took my "hope bracelet," the one I made when mom first got sick, and I threw it into the ocean. Somehow I just felt like I was supposed to let it go. That it was time. And it was okay.

In the fall of 2000, shortly after mom was diagnosed with cancer, our family spent a Sunday afternoon together with the specific task of making "hope bracelets." We got the idea from Kari & her family when Rhonda got sick, and we made them to be a constant reminder to each of us to pray for mom, to pray for each other, and to remind us to never give up hope.

Monday, May 20, 2002
Manteca, CA

Empty
Blank
Unsettled
Compelled
Public places are difficult for me
But I don't want to be at home.

> *"I was terrified that I truly would not survive without her. Not that I'd die, but I'd fall apart."*
> *– Cynthia, age 33*

During the summer of 2001, before I moved back home from California, I remember telling Kelley, "If Mom dies, just go ahead and check me into a mental hospital." The one thing I felt I couldn't survive would be my mother's death. Obviously, as hard as it is, God's grace is truly sufficient. Just as He promised.

Tuesday, May 28, 2002
Manteca, CA

Yesterday was Memorial Day. I didn't do anything.
Sunday night I went with Becky to take "grandpa"
to the hospital. He had a T.I.A., which is a mini
stroke. I didn't know what to do, but I didn't need
to do anything—she just needed someone to go
with her. It was the first time I'd been in a hospital
since mom died. It was a bit strange, but I think I
was okay. The day after, it seemed harder. I
couldn't do anything. It took all my energy just to
sit. And be. And I got sick last night. That same sick
that just hurts my stomach and my chest. I was
awake most all night and so tired. I didn't know,
when I was coming to Becky's, that there was an
older, disabled person in her family. Grandpa is
Becky's sister-in-law's dad. Becky took care of him
on last weekend, which allowed her brother and his
wife to take a mini vacation. Grandpa is really nice.
The whole family is. They've included me in their
family. But I wasn't expecting this. I miss my mom.

Tuesday, May 28, 2002
Manteca, CA

My daddy called me tonight.
He and Keith are coming to see me on June 6!

We are going to Crater Lake in Oregon.
I'm so happy they're coming!
Smile
Smile
Smile

Wednesday, May 29, 2002
Manteca, CA

Today is mmmelancholy.
It's thick and hot out.
The breeze feels like it's coming out of a fireplace.
The sun hangs low in the sky, drawing tall, skinny
shadows over itchy grass.
Car windows are all rolled up with air conditioning
blasting at full-fan.
I'm sitting in Starbucks at a table by the window
watching life go on.
Cars.
Stoplights.
Taillights.
Blinkers.
No afternoon strollers through the park.
Just afternoon drivers in their own little air-
conditioned boxes.
Jazz music seeps into my head and into my
melancholy like a tenor sax.

Uncertain. Unpredictable. But, like me, it has it's own pace and keeps right on going.
If life can't be a beach, it might as well be jazz.

"Always wish that you may find patience enough in yourself to endure, and simplicity enough to believe." – Rainer Maria Rilke

Tuesday, June 18, 2002
Manteca, CA

My pen is running out of ink . . .

For a few days I colored with my Korean crayons. Flowers in all kinds of colors. Colors and crayons. It was good for me.

On Thursday, June 6, the day after my papa's birthday, he and Keith came to visit! I was so happy. The happiest I'd been in months! We drove north. We stopped at Lassen Volcanic Park and took pictures. The next morning we went up to Crater Lake, which was beautiful! So, so blue. Deep, dark, bright blue. Like nothing I can describe. Wow! Snow on the ground and on the mountain peaks. Blue and white—in extremes—and so amazing.

After a brief detour we arrived at the delightful See Vue Motel with our room overlooking the Pacific Ocean. It was gorgeous. We spent the next day driving up and down the Oregon coast, hiking sand dunes and the Hobbit Trail. The sunset was spectacular and we stopped for the night in Portland. After church we drove along the Columbia River Gorge and stopped off at Multnomah Falls. Mount Hood called us for a detour. Back at the hotel, we played cards until it was time to take Keith to the airport. Dad stayed with me and we drove further north, to Seattle. It was a sunny, clear day! We went to Pike Place Market and saw the fish guys throwing fish. We walked all through the market, and stopped for an espresso at the original Starbucks. We walked into town and listened to a street musician play the pan flute. We walked down to the pier and had clam chowder for lunch. The seagulls were flying all around. It was so peaceful. We bought a big bouquet of sweet peas at the market. They really smelled sweet—I had no idea! Their scent filled the car. Tuesday was a long driving day, heading back south. Dad got to meet Becky's whole family before he left on Thursday morning. It was a wonderful, wonderful trip. I love my family!

When I was a little girl, my daddy's nickname for me was Sweet Pea. I don't think I'd ever seen them, or smelled them, before this.

Monday, June 24, 2002
Agricola, Mississippi

I'm at Grandma's :)

There was a BIG family reunion on Saturday. My cousin hosted it over in Alabama down on the Mobile Bay. There were so many people there—over 100. Several distant relatives also came from Georgia. It was a beautiful day, and my biggest surprise was that Keith came too!

I love being here. It's peaceful.

Is this where I'm supposed to stay?

This family reunion was for my mom's side of the family. It was great seeing everyone, including other relatives that I don't usually get to see. One aspect that Keith and I found difficult was that, even though we were surrounded by family, each individual family tended to break into groups. This was the first time we'd been to a family reunion without mom—our

immediate family. We weren't really sure where we "fit."
It was still a wonderful time. This was just
something we hadn't anticipated, but we were able to
adjust.

Summer, 2002

Sunday, June 30, 2002
Starbucks – Pacific Beach, CA

And then I cried.
Miss-her tears.
Blue skies and sunshine. Foofy clouds. Starbucks
and palm trees. Moody music. And tears.

A mom just walked over to a table, handed her
daughter flowers and said, "Happy birthday."

My birthday is in three days and I don't have a
mom anymore.

*Becky and I took another trip down to southern
California to see some friends. I had no idea that
my first birthday without mom was going to be so*

incredibly difficult. It was definitely one of my most difficult days as I worked through my grief.

Monday, July 1, 2002
Pacific Beach, CA

Yesterday was a crying day. We went to church and then to Starbucks and I just couldn't stop crying. Oh, I just missed her so much. We went back to Kevin's and I slept for four hours. That was necessary. When Kevin came home we went out on the balcony and sat. Becky was asleep. I talked. He listened. I talked about feeling "homeless." he said, "Home is where you know you'll never be turned away."

Saturday, July 6, 2002
Manteca, CA

Becky's family took me out to dinner at the Olive Garden to celebrate my 36th birthday tonight. Chris, Becky's sister-in-law made me a gorgeous quilt in blue and yellow with stars—my absolute favorite colors! I love it so much!

Friday, July 12, 2002
Manteca, CA

"I'll be happy when I know you're writing
everyday," Keith said.
"Okay buddy. I'll try harder."
I love my brother.

*Keith called me often while I was in California. He
was my best friend at the time, and we were going
through this experience together, even though we were far
apart. Often, when he called we wouldn't even talk—
sometimes for an hour or more. We didn't really have
anything to say. We just didn't want to be alone with
our thoughts and memories.*

Sunday, July 14, 2002
Manteca, CA

Today is six months.
I miss her so much!

Cali Gail Girl . . . you'll be okay . . .

Wednesday, July 17, 2002
Manteca, CA

Today is melancholy, but not sad.

Tuesday, July 22, 2002
Manteca, CA

It was a large envelope. Red, white, and blue.
Priority mail, it said. And my name was on it. From
Keith, my brother, for my birthday, and I smiled.
"Rip" it said as I tore the pull strip off the envelope.
Now it's open. I pull out the package. It's wrapped
in glossy black & white paper—a photo of school
children standing on the steps for their class
picture. They're fourth grade. It doesn't say this
anywhere, but I can just tell. It's a thin package. I
peel the tape carefully so I don't rip the glossy
picture-paper that it's wrapped in. One end is
already open. Hmm. I pull out a cinnamon-colored
book, wrapped again in a clear plastic sleeve. I pull
the book from the sleeve. I'm actually touching it.
It's here, in my hands. I flip through carefully while
my friends sit down to lunch, not at all
understanding my fascination or my joy. This book
contains words. Words I'm hungry for. Not because
I've read this book, but because I've read the author
and his words touched me and inspired me, even

long before I met the man and really, before I truly heard his music for the first time. I gently carry the book to the other room and I smile. Smiles are rare these days because my heart is broken. My dear mother died, and I wait for God to heal my heart because He is the only one who can. But today, I smile, and I wait. For the day to end. For the sun to set. For the windows to be open. For the breeze to be cool. For the world to go to sleep. And now it's time. The wind stirs the leaves and they sing to me. My blanket comforts me. And my heart smiles. It is time to read *Unsung* by Linford Detweiler of Over the Rhine.

I read four and a half pages, and then I got out of bed and sent my brother an email:

My dear brother . . . you have given me a gift. One that made me get out of bed, after writing the above in my journal just before I opened and started reading it. And four and a half pages in, I had to stop and thank you . . . so you would know . . . how much I love you.

May I excerpt a few phrases from the book so you can understand?

   "We will write these days down together . . . the pages we write will help us to be born many times.

The chapters we write will teach us that we believe in miracles . . . "

"We will write with no fear of breaking our hearts, our hearts are already broken."

"What are we to do with the infinity found in a single day or night? Is the light of early morning a burden we must bear? Do the mountains hum, the rocks cry out?"

So Keith . . . I will no longer pass the hours in a day, longing for it to pass because it is another day. (Okay, maybe I'll still have days like these, but I choose to aspire to embrace the "infinity found in a single day or night.") I will write. I will paint. I will color. As best as I can because I am not dead . . . I am still alive . . . and I will be me, as best as I can. When I think I don't know who I am, I will cling to what I do know, in my soul, and that is, I am creative, and I need to get it out.

I love you brother,
Your big sister,
Calondra Gail Ludlow
Writer and artist

This was a real turning point for me. It was the first time I really knew that I was going to be okay.

That my life would go on. I felt I had a purpose again, even if that purpose was simply to continue living.

The Next Year

"I'm willing to fight for my life. I want it back."

*"We will write to go about the work of
saving our lives."*

– Linford Detweiler, Over the Rhine

Yes . . . I am taking my life back. I choose life! This
life that my mother gave me.

*I moved back down to southern California and
began the task of looking for a job and looking for a
place of my own to live. I was moving forward again.
In the fall, however, God made it very clear to me
that His plan for me was to move back to Virginia,
near my family. I moved in with my brother, Keith.
Right back into the same bedroom that I had moved
out of when I moved to California in 2000.*

The days have their stories, but from this point on I'm choosing to share only the parts of my journal that I feel were significant in the healing process, as it continued over the next year. Remember, it's a process. It's a journey.

"It's all right. You have to go all the way through your feelings before you can come out on the other side. But don't stay where you are . . . move on."
– Madeline L'Engle in <u>A House Like a Lotus</u>

Thursday, August 15, 2002
Encinitas, CA

I said it out loud a couple of times today, " . . . just after my mother died . . . " some days it doesn't really seem real. But it is. So here I am. Looking. Being. Praying. Listening. Yes, even still, waiting.

Tuesday, August 20, 2002
Orange County, CA

The air smells different here. You can tell, even though you can't see it or hear it. You can smell it in the air. Kind of like snow in the winter, but nothing like snow in the winter. It doesn't snow here. But you can smell it in the air. The ocean. I'm near the ocean.

The sky is grey. The air is cool, and warm, all at once. I think it's a bit more humid today than usual, and that's taken the chill off. Either way, it's comfortable.

I've looked at many. Read chapters of some. I'm always drawn to them, but I'd never bought one, until today. A book about loss, about grief. This one is 23 years old, but this one just seemed to say it best. So I bought it, and I'm taking it home with me. It is *Don't Take Away My Grief*, by Doug Manning.

You know how it feels when you get a pill stuck in your throat and it won't go down? My throat felt that way all day yesterday. But there wasn't anything stuck.

Excerpt from my Christmas letter, 2002

My mom, Sara, went home to heaven on January 14th this year. I miss her. And my life is forever different without her here. But I know that her absence from her body resulted in her presence with the Lord, and that's got to be a wonderful place to be. There's comfort in knowing I'll see her again . . . but honestly, sometimes that comfort seems an awfully long way away. It's been a hard year. Very introspective. But God is still good, all the time, and I'd rather trust Him with my life than live it any other way.

Saturday, January 11, 2003
Reston, VA

Hot tears pour in streams down my cheeks. Salty and wet. Yet there's comfort in the warmth. Comfort in release. Comfort in tears.

The air catches in my throat. It blocks my words and will not allow their sounds to escape. Such a strong, invisible barrier, trapping my words in thought alone.

And the price I pay in releasing the words is tears, as I choke on the air. As it mixes with the sounds. And slowly, deliberately, verbal expression happens.

I find it takes much more energy to allow the words to come out than it takes to simply keep the tears in. Reminds me of a quote I knew long ago that spoke of salt water being healing: tears, the ocean, sweat.

Sunday, February 9, 2003
Reston, VA

Don't talk when writing will do.

It's been a weekend of words. Many writers. Many quotes. Many things said that stuck. Their ideas anyway. Melancholy music. Frustrated feelings. Unknowing. Uncertain. Uneasy. Unsure.

When you're surrounded by words and books and thoughts and ideas it is both inspiring and intimidating. I spent some time in the bookstore. Hadn't done that in a while. Need to do it more. Get into the thought, the way, the practice of reading and writing words. It's a good thing. Necessary. It's like an oxymoron, or a dichotomy about the inspiration and intimidation of being surrounded by authors. Good and not so good.

Then just snippets. Not whole books . . . not a long enough attention span for that. I think I'm in the middle of about five books right now, and not really working on finishing any of them. Just muddling through them in small bites. Tasty, but I'm not really hungry for them. Because when you get hungry for an author, you can't stop reading. Its like it just possesses you. Maybe my soul is looking to be possessed by some inspiration and finding the current list of reads lacking. Picked up Eugene Peterson's *The Message* yesterday. I'm sure that its probably the inspiration my soul is longing for and that's why everything else seems void.

I want to read more. I want to write more. I want to create with a sense of purpose. Why is it that these things that are so necessary are so difficult? It's like trying to breathe under water. You can see the surface. You can even stick your fingers out of the water. You just can't quite seem to get there and breathe. Maybe I'm just not trying hard enough. Maybe I just don't want it bad enough. Maybe. Whatever.

Monday, February 10, 2003
Reston, VA

I don't understand the uneasiness. The restlessness. I don't know what else to call it. I can't really find words that describe it and I find the effort spent trying to be almost overwhelming. Its like I need to

move on to something else . . . get over it.
Somehow writing about my uncertain feelings is
my way of working through them so I can come
out on the other side.

Wednesday would have been mom's 61st birthday.
We—Dad, Keith, Norman, Erin and I—are spending
part of the day together. I think we're going to the
cemetery. Then to lunch, because mom liked to go
out to eat. And we will have cake, because mom
loved having birthday cake. Whew. She's been in
heaven for just over a year now. I know she has no
idea how long, because time is different up there.
Or maybe it simply doesn't exist. I don't know.
Some days I feel as though I'm doing quite well . . .
in working through my feelings. And other days it
seems just as new and painful. Loss is a deep hurt
that takes a long time to heal. Because healing has
to occur at so many different levels.

I find that music is simultaneously soothing and
painful. It comforts me because it speaks to my
soul. But my soul is what is wounded so it is very
tender. Sometimes music is just too potent. Certain
books are the same way.

This past weekend was an empty brain weekend.
Whenever someone asked me what I was thinking
there was just nothing there. Completely empty. I
needed to create. I carved two rubber stamps. Both

flowers. A tulip, and another obscure flower whose name I don't know. There is satisfaction in creating, but I still felt empty. It is very frustrating to need something . . . and try to fulfill that need . . . only to still feel so unfulfilled upon its completion. I know that sounds vague but I don't know how else to explain it.

I spent a lot of time this weekend reading. Bits and pieces. Authors that were familiar. Quotes I knew. Looking for comfort there. Yes, there was some, but I came away even more frustrated, needing to do my own writing and not feeling capable or adequate. Feeling inferior. I ached inside listening to the language of these writers. I've been touched, but not satisfied by their words. I need to turn to the Scripture to be satisfied. To read God's words. To look there for comfort. I say He is all I really need. I believe it, but I desperately want to feel it. I want to feel it. Please, touch me.

Thursday, February 27, 2003
Reston, VA

> *"Live your life and every day you breathe, just enjoy it. And enjoy those around you as much as you can." – Barry Watson*

Life is . . .   At any given moment there are probably over a million true ways to finish that sentence.

Friday, March 21, 2003
Clearwater, FL

I don't know why I've always been captivated by the ocean. I can't explain why it touches my soul so deeply. I may never understand why I'm so drawn to it. But I know, with sand under my toes and the cold waves crashing over my feet, that everything is going to be okay. And that makes me a very lucky girl.

Monday, March 24, 2003
Reston, VA

I've been making myself go out every day. That's good for me. In the past eleven days I've only stayed in one of those days. I was getting stuck staying home or indoors. Didn't want to go outside. Just showered and put on clean pajamas again. The sunshine is good and necessary, and I'm consciously working to make sure I get out in it a bit every day.

Wednesday, March 26, 2003
Suffolk, VA

460 East is a four-lane highway and it was just such a lovely, meandering drive. Sunny day. Convertible top down. Wind in the hair. Good music on the stereo. Singing at the top of my lungs. Great day. What was most obvious during that stretch of the drive was the color. Virginia is a generally colorful state, but winter in Virginia is so very bland. The first thing I noticed was a certain type of tree. It's not that the trees were budding and popping out with little sprigs of green. Most of them were still winter drab grey. But these particular trees were like big white fuzz balls! Just billows of white, everywhere, like giant cumulus clouds. Bradford Pear trees, so I'm told. I'd heard of them, of course, but had no idea what they looked like and that they were so spectacular in the spring. How did I not notice them before? And then, driving along, I noticed the yellow. This one, I knew well. Forsythia. Another one of those plants that just all of a sudden pop out in screaming color. "Notice me!" they yell. And it's hard not to! And then I started paying closer attention. And yes, all over the place were little hints that spring is, indeed, here. Daffodils in yellow and white . . . the first flowers to poke their little heads up through the ground. And in my friend's front yard, so little and perfect they looked like fake flowers, purple crocus. Crocuses.

Croci. What's the plural? The plural of my one hour drive down 460 east was spring, and what a place to be!

Monday, July 21, 2003
Reston, VA

Hazy, hot and humid. At least there is sunshine. Better than the days and days of rain. Vitamin D— the sun is the best source.

I feel ungrounded again today. Nothing's wrong . . . just everything's not quite right. Or maybe this is just how things are now. This feeling . . . it's just a kind of day I didn't used to have, but now I do. Part of the repertoire of days in my life. It's similar to the foggy days, but not quite the same. On those days I just couldn't focus. On these days, I just feel like I'm floating. My mind is just scattered, like a breeze blew through it. And I go to pick up the pieces of thoughts and try to put them back and then I realize that they are . . . blank? I want to live in the moment but the moment is empty. I want to have goals for my future, but I can't see past the moment. The bland, empty, now of my life. I am not dissatisfied with my life. Nor with myself . . . who I am. I just don't know anything. The physical act of being must be enough for now.

Sunday, August 31, 2003
Reston, VA

Labor Day weekend. The so-called end of summer.
It's been a busy one. I've not been home much
over the past few months. I've helped plan, and
have been in three weddings this year, and now the
weddings are over. Everyone else is moving on to
whatever is next.

I'm home again. Here. Trying to make sense of it
all. And not succeeding too well. I am depressed. If
I could only sleep, I probably would. I go from
busy, busy, and busy to stopped, stuck and sleepy.
Maybe that's why I've stayed gone so much lately.
Will I ever be at peace in my own home again? Oh,
I do hope so.

I've lost it. I keep losing important things.

I've lost Keith.

It's not the same anymore. We're just stuck. Stuck.
I've lost my friend. We don't have anything to say
anymore. Our brains are both stuck, and we can't
decide. I think he spends most of his time frustrated
with me. I can't help him figure anything out. We
can't even decide simple things, like what to eat. It's
like they just don't matter. Weekends are hard
enough. Long weekends are just . . . harder longer.

And my throat is sore.

And I feel like a failure in so many ways and on so many levels.

Thursday, September 25, 2003
Reston, VA

Writing is necessary on the bad days. It's boring on the good days. The writing . . . not life. The good days of life keep me moving on. Going forward. Living.

Well, Keith and I seem to have worked through the muck. It's been much better. I cried that Sunday night, long and hard, and then my head hurt. I slept hard and on Monday we talked. He said, "Have you read *Ruthless Trust?*" I told him, "I started it three years ago but didn't get very far." "Read it," he said. So I did. And I struck gold on page 12, where Brennan Manning said:

> *The way of trust is a movement into obscurity, into the undefined, into ambiguity, not into some predetermined, clearly delineated plan for the future. The next step discloses itself only out of a discernment of God acting in the desert of the present moment. The reality of naked*

*trust is the life of a pilgrim who leaves what is
nailed down, obvious, and secure, and walks
into the unknown without any rational
explanation to justify the decision or guarantee
the future. Why? Because God has signaled the
movement and offered it his presence and his
promise.*

*Of course there were days when I was afraid,
when my heart sank and my body trembled,
when I felt muddled and befuddled, when I felt
like a bewildered child alone and lost in the
dark night, hearing strange and frightening
noises; put simply, there were days when
anxiety and uncertainty prevailed. Then out of
nowhere came a calm, reassuring voice, "Do
not be afraid, I am with you."*

I finished the book two days ago. It was chock-full
of gold nuggets. So much so that I didn't want to
rush through it and miss them. I read deliberately.
Slowly. I read with a pen. I bought the book three
years ago, but God knew that I would need it now,
much more than I wanted it then, so He shelved it
for a few years until I really needed it. He does
things like that.

So here I am. Growing. Trusting, as best I can.
Going along my way, one step at a time as God
shows them to me. Knowing that He's right here by

my side because He loves me. Loves me too much to leave me where I am. Loves me too much to leave me the way I am. I think there are many similarities between the way trust feels and the way grief feels. I think they both change your life forever. Change is scary. Change is hard. Changed by God is necessary. I choose the way of trust. It is the only way. This I know.

Made in the USA
Charleston, SC
19 July 2012